Welcome to the World of

Happy Pants

GW00776097

PUFFIN BOOKS

I wake up in the morning
As happy as can be
As long as I can make myself
A nice hot mug of tea!

I've got some posters in my room
And pics of hunky boys
But my bed is also piled high
With cute and fluffy toys!

I'm putting on my lip gloss
My bracelets and my rings
Cos Happy Pants loves nothing more
Than wearing gorgeous things!

I've only got one weakness -
I really love the phone
Cos chatting to my mates all day
Makes me feel right at home!

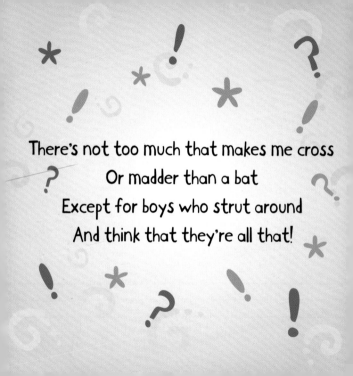

There's not too much that makes me cross
Or madder than a bat
Except for boys who strut around
And think that they're all that!

I like to get together
And go out with my mates
We shop and we go bowling
And we cruise on rollerskates!

Watching soaps on telly
Is my favourite thing to do
While eating yummy pizza
And a little cake or two!

It's fun to go out grooving
But after a long day
I love a gorgeous bubble bath
To soak my cares away.